The Event Marketing Playbook
Everything You'll Ever Need to Know About Events

Author: Adella Pasos

Are you interested in learning how event marketing can improve your business and profits? Tired of getting nowhere fast? The event marketing playbook is a strategic guide that explains how to set up, promote and profit from events.

Whether you are planning events for a nightclub, conference, trade show, executive retreat, golf outing, corporate or customer appreciation events, company dinner, holiday party, fundraising gala, team building events or even product launch events, this book will teach you how to create events that attract new customers, referrals and a consistent flow of business that you can rely on.

D1571316

The Event Marketing Playbook
Everything You'll Ever Need to Know About Events

Published by Adella Pasos
Copyright © 2020 www.adellapasos.com

Table of Contents

Table of Contents Continued...

Chapter 6: Generating Publicity and Exposure for Your Event

This chapter discusses the top 8 strategies corporations use to generate more exposure for their events and a practical event marketing timeline.

Chapter 7: Using Social Media to Promote Your Event

This chapter reveals the 5 ways to engage with your audience and promote your event using social media only. The top 6 methods for organic and paid social media marketing are explained.

Chapter 8: Best Ways to Generate More Money on Event Day

This chapter explains 10 ways to increase revenue and monetize your event on the day of the event. It reveals a list of products and services you can sell to get more money.

Chapter 9: Event Marketing Resources

This chapter includes a list of impressive event marketing templates and systems for events. So you can design beautiful event campaigns to effectively communicate with your audience and share your message.

Appendix: Frequently Asked Questions

This is a great spot to check out the most common questions people have about other ways to make money and benefits of event marketing.

Introduction: About This E-Book

Hello! and thanks for downloading this awesome book. Throughout the course of this book you will learn how to get paid by using simple strategies to create, promote and profit events. I wrote this book for you to truly see that legit money can be made and it doesn't have to be done through a get rich quick scheme.

The strategies that I've listed in the book will explain how you can get paid from using event marketing, as well as where and how to get started. Entrepreneurs, start-ups, and even large fortune 500 companies are using the same strategies to gain millions of dollars. So, where's your piece of the pie? Who doesn't love a fast track to success?

Who am I?

I am an International Business Coach and Marketing Strategist who has shared my passion for growing brands from the ground up. I've worked with startups, small businesses, global corporations and entertainment talent that recognize the value of marketing. I give my clients the ability to sell more by preparing them with the right strategies in social media, mobile, merchandising, and events. Providing simple solutions to complex challenges, I've placed all that I know into these books.

Now, it's time for you to apply the knowledge, and get out there and put your game face on!

Cheers to your success,

Adella Pasos

Chapter 1: Event Marketing Basics

Why Event Marketing?

Whether you've launched a new brand or you have an existing brand, the importance of event marketing is still the same. The number one reason brands organize events is to strengthen their brand's position in the marketplace.

Events allow you to easily promote your products, services or your cause on-site or online. It has an unlimited potential to help you build relationships with the people who matter the most. It also allows you to generate leads from interested prospects and engage with your customers in a more interactive, personable way. If you are looking to profit off of events or just expand your brand's presence and sales opportunities, this book was written with you in mind.

How Event Marketing Helps

Events provide attendees with a valuable opportunity to form a bond with your brand. Here are 10 ways event marketing can help your business:

Increase Sales
Generate Leads
Expand your network
Convey your message
Send qualified traffic to your website
Get more appointments and bookings
Collect feedback & insights
Create new streams of income

What are the Benefits of Event Marketing?

If your brand is having a hard time reaching a target audience, or generating traffic and sales, event marketing has a big advantage over many other strategies. Not only will event marketing give you the opportunity to direct sales, but also opens up conversations that allow you to educate your prospects and customers. The main benefits are:

- Grow your brand with partnerships and sponsorships
- Events can be thrown 24 hours a day, 365 days a year
- Reliable tools are available for promotion and tracking
- People actually remember events and experiences
- Opens up an opportunity to demo products and sell on-demand

How Do I Start?

Step 1: Establish Your Event Goals and Budget

The first step is deciding on the main goal of your event. It can be multiple goals for example: to collect leads, to sell and take orders, to meet and greet with decision makers, to collect feedback from attendees, etc. Then decide on how much you can afford to make that happen.

Step 2: Brand Your Event - Pick a Name, Logo and Make it Unique

The next step is to 'brand' your event. Pick a name for the event and make it memorable, exciting and specific. Get a logo created for the event. I prefer to use 99designs for marketing design work, they are always the most reliable.

Step 3: Organize the Logistics and Pick a Location

After you've got your logo and brand established, next you'll need to contact venues for pricing of their location. Be very specific and prepared to communicate the date/s of the event, how long you will need the space, how many attendees you expect, and if you'll need any furniture, lighting or electrical hookups, or to rent their audio / video equipment. Collect quotes and decide on which location fits into your budget.

Step 4: Get Sponsorships & Choose Vendors

After you've paid your deposit on the venue, it's time to sell sponsorships to help pay for all the other expenses you'll need to throw the event. Be sure to create a sponsorship pricing and package list that you can email to interested brands and vendors. Popular packages include silver, gold and platinum sponsorship levels.

You can get this document designed at **99designs,** too. Choose to work with vendors and brands whose presence will compliment the type of event you are throwing. Also, be prepared to fully deliver all that is promised in your sponsorship agreement.

Step 5: Promote Event & Accept Payments

There are many methods to promote your events, but the first thing you need to do is make your tickets easy to buy online. Many beginners will opt to create a custom branded website, which can be purchased through **99designs.**

You can also set up a quick registration page through a website like Eventbrite.com. When you promote, make sure your ads and promotions are exposed in places where your target market is. The banners should be posted on their favorite blogs, magazines, news sites, public places and more. Don't forget about social media and using influencers to help spread via word of mouth, too!

How Do I Get Paid?

You will easily earn money with event marketing by doing any of the following below. The biggest takeaway here is **you need to SELL!**

- selling tickets at different price levels, like early bird and late registration
- selling sponsorships
- sell vendor booths spaces
- selling advertising placements
- selling merchandise and gear for the event
- selling limited edition or commemorative products selling photos at the event
- selling access to wifi
- selling VIP parking and VIP seating
- sell special pre-event premium experiences VIP tickets
- sell mastermind or coaching programs as apart of the event
- selling up-graded ticket options
- selling exclusive meet and greet packages
- selling ads on your website to vendors / sponsors
- selling naming rights for awards given away at the events
- selling speaking opportunities at the event
- selling promotional announcements at the event selling dvd or online recordings of the event
- sell access to a special luncheon or dinner
- sell access to a live stream of the event
- sell access to a refreshment room where people can take a break
- create an event app with itinerary and sell ads on it

conduct a survey and sell sponsorships for that

giveaway awards and sell sponsorships on those

create a game for attendees to play and sell sponsors on that

Sell access to the final attendees email list

Event Marketing Best Practices

Here is a list of key things to remember that will help you along the way.

1) Set realistic goals & budgets

Be specific when deciding on a goal and budget. Choose a flat number and move forward with what you have while you work on obtaining sponsors. You can always increase the marketing efforts once you have a plan and budget in place.

Once you know your budget, start setting up the marketing goals. Don't be afraid to pick a target group of people who would be interested in attending or give it serious thought. Setting up a event breaks down to asking yourself a few key questions:

- How many people do I want or need to reach?
- How much time do I have to reach them?
- Do we need food, drinks or refreshments?
- What kind of venue would best suit this event?
- Do I currently have the abilities or resources to make this happen?
- Is my goal to sell products, obtain signups, educate or entertain?
- How much should I spend on marketing?

2) Make a creative theme

People attending your event want to know what it's all about. Choosing a theme sets the tone for the event and makes it more memorable. Examples could be: Back to School, Great Gatsby, Mythical Creatures, Luau, Willy Wonka, Graffiti, Black and White, International, Mardi Gras, Jungle, 80s or 90s. It's important to know your audience.

For corporate events or sales meetings, I would recommend choosing a theme that the stakeholders and speakers can get excited about and feel connected to. Example themes would be: "Building for the Future, Anything is Possible, Challenge Yourself, Expect the Best, Great Expectations, Grow Your Business, Leadership: Share the Vision, Navigating the Future, Shoot for the Stars, The Power of Performance, Do Great Things. A little thought can go a long way. Don't forget to jazz it up and have a little fun.

3) Create a promotional timeline

Who will be responsible for event marketing? Normally, if you are the planner and organizer, the job is yours. If you have room in your budget to pay for a marketer, a helpful tip would be to work side by side to map out a promotional timeline. It's important to create a timeline from start to finish to accurately promote any event. You want to give yourself enough time for people to make a decision on attending and really penetrate your target audience.

Starting 3 months before your event, you should sort out all your pre-event activities, get the event website ready, decide on your social media announcements, email outreach, any promotional giveaways or early bird promo start and end dates, blog postings, social influencer outreach, decide on partners to help promote and what kind of advertising you will be doing. Don't wait till the last minute, prices will rise. ***You'll need to make every dollar work for you at your event.***

4) Sell Sponsorships to Fill the Gaps

You want to get as much buy-in as possible and increase stakeholders. Securing sponsorships is not always the easiest task for event organizers, but a crucial one to produce a large scale event. Before you reach out to sponsors, you'll need to prepare an attractive sponsorship package for them to buy. Since you are organizing an event, it's common practice to remind them of who you are, what the event is for, and how they will benefit.

The top reason a sponsor would want to give you money and buy your packages is the ability to get their brand, products, or services in front of a large number of people all at once.

When building a sponsorship package, there's lots of opportunities that you can offer them: sales leads, potential traffic to their social media pages, their brand name mentioned all over the event, banners with their logo everywhere in sight, maybe it's something as simple as a cookie that is given out to every attendee with their brand's name and website on the wrapper.

Your event gives them a good chance to put their business front and center. You can also include them in all the media exposure. Leveraging sponsorships gets you more money in your pockets and the ability to leverage partners to help co-promote and bring in even more people to the event.

5) Pay attention to attendance numbers and revenue

Your #1 goal with each event is to drive interest, fill the room and get sales. You'll need to bring enough revenue to cover all expenses for the event. Here are a few things you'll need to include in your event budget:

- Equipment rentals, venue costs, entertainment costs
- Advertising costs, video production costs,
- Graphic design fees, name badges, programs, event signage
- Giveaway items, security deposit, extra insurance, wifi,
- Balloons, lighting, candles, tablecloths, speakers, alcohol
- Food, shuttle service, swag bags, promotional items, meals
- Hotels, temporary event or serving staff

This is just a "short list" of what your revenue will actually need to cover. If you plan on making profit from the events, you'll need to pay close attention to how many people are registered, monitor your attendance numbers and figure out where you can always up-sell more, add additional packages or increase sponsorship revenue.

These key things will help you increase attendance quickly:

- Cross promote your event with other organizations
- Email your current attendees with a referral incentive
- Require speakers to help promote the event within their own networks
- Promote online in groups and on social media
- Create a last minute ticket discount offer
- Launch a paid ad campaign to generate last minute sales
- Promote a 2 for one deal, for example, if they buy one ticket, they can bring a friend for 1/2 off the second ticket.

Chapter 2: How to Set Event Goals

How to Make an Event Action Plan

What do you plan on achieving with your event? Do you want more customers, get more leads or is it a means to communicate company updates or milestones? Each event requires a different organizational goal structure.

You'll need to make sure the goals are specific, can be measured, that you have what it takes to achieve the goals, make sure the goals focus on the right results, and have a target completion date. To set up the goals, you just need to ask yourself, what is your current state and what is your desired state? Here's why you need goals:

To help you identify resources needed to accomplish work

To clarify how work is and should be accomplished
To confirm what needs to get done

To help make the job easier and more meaningful

To help increase the likelihood that results will be achieved

Here's a list of specific event goals for example:

We want to increase awareness about the launch of our new program by the end of July.
We want to increase leads by 40% this month. We want to increase funding by 25% this quarter.
We want to share our presentation with 200 people at the event.

We want to collect over 250 new names and phone numbers by next week.

We want to setup at least 5 decision maker meetings by the end of the event

We want to sample our product to at least 500 people at the end of the event.

We want to collect feedback from over 900 people by the event.

We want to sell at least 20 units each hour at the event.

We want to get our brochure in the hands of over 250 people

We want to recruit 15 new employees by the end of the event

Now that you know your goals, it's time to take action to make those things happen. Start with the goal and map it back to a strategy, then an objective and the tactic to get it done.

For example:

Goal: Make $15,000 net from ticket sales and reduce catering costs

Strategy: Hiring more sales team members to add new sponsors

Objective: Increase Ticket Price by $15, Reduce Food Costs by $5

Tactics: Revisit menu and see where cuts can be made, find new food vendor or renegotiate, increase # volunteers for the event, create incentives for them to sell tickets, require a sales team to sell at least 15- 20 tickets a week, identify top corporations in the area who may be interested in sponsorship opportunities, create top level advertisement opportunities for new sponsors only.

Chapter 3: Booking Venues & Hiring Help

First things first, venue sourcing can take a lot of time, but once you have confirmed your event's city / location. **You can simply go to google.com and search " event venues near [city name] or [zip   code]". This will usually reveal a large list of results.**

Most website's will allow you to browse and get rental pricing for thousands of event venues fast. Please allow yourself two to three different date options, because not all venues will have the dates available. You will want to fill out the inquiry form online, or to expedite the process, go ahead and jump on a call and ask to speak with the venue's event coordinator.

I like to use CVent. They have over 200,000 destinations across the globe. When requesting a proposal you'll need to know the answers to the following questions up front:

1. How many people does the room need to hold?

2. Do you need food and beverages / catering?

3. Will you need tables / chairs / linens?

4. Do you need a setup / clean up crew?

5. Will you need a bar / alcohol served?

6. Will you need audio / visual / wifi capabilities?

7. Do you have a specific size booth or space requirement?

8. Will you need insurance for the event?

9. Do you need special accessibility accommodation?

10. How much parking will you need?

Depending on the type of event you are putting on, here are some general event space ideas that may accommodate your group:

- Art Galleries & Museums
- NightClubs & Lounges
- Wineries & Farmhouses
- Rooftop Gardens, Restaurants
- Cafes Hotels & Yacht Clubs
- Golf Course or Country Club
- Banquet Hall Conference Center Stadiums
- Lodge / Warehouse
- Theatres / Co-Work Facilities
- Church / Chapel

When it comes to organizing and hiring a team, make sure you'll have enough event staff to cover the event. Many of these people can be hired via short term contract through a local agency. **Search google for terms like "short term event staff" or "event staffing [city name]". You may need to hire these types of people:**

1. Ticket Sales Reps
2. Volunteers (if needed)
3. Promotional Models
4. Hostess
5. Coat Check Team
6. Demonstrators
7. Sign spinners / Costume Characters
8. Wait Staff
9. Cashiers
10. Setup / Breakdown Logistic Teams
11. Bartenders or Baristas
12. Registration Staff
13. Team Leaders / Supervisors
14. Dancers / Comedians / Live Entertainment
15. Game Booth Attendees

Once you get your venue sorted out, staff confirmed the last thing to do is review your deliverables. Create a spreadsheet with a list of the items you've ordered or set in place and make sure everything is running on time and according to schedule.

If you ordered flyers for the event? Ensure there is a delivery date, if there are times setup for staff to attend training, make sure the list is confirmed and times are set in stone, if you ordered a few games or props, make sure the pickup times are all synced in a calendar and there are no loose ends. It's essential to make sure you update the status of each deliverable whether they are in progress, quality reviewed, have been accepted, and then finally delivered.

Chapter 4: Event Management Systems

Eventbrite is one of the most popular online ticketing systems used by small businesses and entrepreneurs. Their platform is a big event search engine for the entire globe. It allows you to list your event, accept ticket sales and event promote via social media. It's a super easy to use platform that allows you to start making sales in minutes. You can list your event for free, but they take 2% + $.79 per ticket sold on their most basic selling package. Check their website for the most updated information.

Bizzabo is one of the world's most popular event ticketing systems for those who need a more robust solution. Bizzable integrates with over 750 platforms like mailchimp, salesforce, slack and more. They have advanced analytics so you can dig into exactly what's going on when people are hitting your sales page. The cost is not provided up front, you must request a demo & pricing. This platform is marketed towards those who put on multiple medium to large scale events per year.

Thunder tix has all of the same options as above, but they also have event management tools like barcode & ticket scanning, season package setup, group discount setup, guest list management, merchandise sales, post-event survey management, general and reserved seating accommodation, cash sales and comped ticket management, donations management and more.

My Recommendation: There are hundreds of others out there. Find a solution that allows you to create a beautiful registration page, that matches your brand, collect payments online, manage your event attendees, use social media marketing promotion, and has analytic reports for you to review stats and updates.

Chapter 5: Identifying Sponsorships & Partnerships

Getting sponsors is your biggest key to making an event sensational and also securing the funding you need to advertise and promote the event. A sponsor could be an individual, small company, midsize or large enterprise corporation. A sponsorship is essentially when they give you money or donate free product or services to support the event or activities at the event, usually in exchange for publicity.

Why Would They Give You Money?

Most sponsors want to know how giving the money or free product will help improve or grow their business. Here's a list of reasons they should sponsor your event:

They get to build trust within a certain demographic or community

They get to engage with potential customers

It helps improve employee engagement by getting them involved

It allows hundreds or thousands of people to see their logo and learn about their brand

It helps them to cut out prospecting time

Helps them increase the number of meetings and bookings

Allows them to complete a goodwill initiative

Allows them to enhance their company image

Helps them differentiate themselves from competitors

It will enhance and strengthen their networking opportunities

It will increase credibility and make people feel comfortable buying

How Does Sponsorship Work?

A sponsor pays a business or individual to promote their brand at the event. This sponsorship can be in the form of direct ads, content promotion, banners, mentions in the event program, ads on the event website, ads on the events social media pages, company name of giveaway gift bags or more.

It's similar to when an athlete does a commercial for a fitness brand, wearing the company's workout clothes while he or she plays. They are paying that athlete to say their brand name and promote it to their audience and followers.

How to Get Sponsors for an Event

Prepare a list of potential local businesses, corporate businesses in the area that would have interest in marketing to your event's audience. Reach out via phone and email to gauge interest. Be excited and ready to sell them on the experience.

Company Overview - Start with a story, tell who you are, the purpose of the event and your mission. You need to create a professionally branded sponsorship kit and make it into a pdf.

Create Benefits - Make sure you have really great benefits for the sponsor and make the package sound irresistible.They want to know how they will benefit from giving you money and this relationship.

Outline the Demographics - Sponsors want to hear about where and to whom their brand will be communicated to. They also want to know what kind of people are attending the event.

Sell the Exposure - Describe how many followers you have, how many hits to your website you have each month, how many names on your email list, who are your partners, and who are the attendees. For example: Are they small business owners, engineering professionals, c-level executives, designers, entrepreneurs, etc. Sponsors need to understand the level of exposure they are getting in exchange for their payment.

Review Deliverables - Seek out the right person from the start. You must ask to speak with the decision maker (usually the marketing department chief, marketing officer or event marketing team, sometimes the owner or ceo of the company) in order to get to the person who writes the checks.

Offer incentives - If a sponsor pays upfront or by a certain deadline offer them a discount. Also, don't be afraid to ask for the money, you'll need as much cash flow upfront as possible to cover event related expenses before launch. Be sure to have your payment accounts setup and ready to receive funds.

Chapter 6: Generating Publicity and Exposure for Your Event

Here are excellent strategies used to generate exposure:

Partner with a non-for-profit cause or offer to donate a percentage of the proceeds to charity. Use this new partnership as leverage to contact local news media outlets to promote the event and good will initiative.

Invite media personalities to take part in the event, not just cover it.

Put out a large press release describing something different and cool about your event, maybe the decor is themed, you have special props or activities or have invited special musicians or celebrities will be there for a meet and greet.

Support a current trend or current event in either fashion or media / pop culture through your event.

Share Inspirational stories of overcoming major challenges or have those people attend your event to share their story and report this to local newspapers and media.

Recognize someone of importance for an award at your event and report it to the media.

Invite Influencers to attend your event and do a VIP experience and have them share it with their fans / followers.

Invite a local celebrity or athlete and invite the first 50 customers to a meet and greet, signing or giveaway and have tv / radio the media covers the event.

Your Event Marketing Timeline

Here's a list of things you need to do before the day of the event.

Month 1

- Establish Goals & Budget
- Decide on an Event Name
- Get Logo & Website Designed
- Choose an Event Theme

- Setup Social Media
- Search for Venues
- Pay Deposit on Venue

Month 2

- Get a Sponsorship Package PDF designed
- Choose a Ticketing System
- Create Daily Social Media
- Choose an Email Provider

- Setup Ad Campaigns
- Decide on Partnerships
- Contact & Follow up with Potential Sponsors
- Capture & Call Leads

Month 3

- Focus on Selling More Sponsorships
- Pay any Equipment Rental or Entertainment costs
- Pay for Giveaways, Balloons, and Food and Beverage

- Hire Temporary Staff
- Send out last minute reminders
- Confirm event signage and
- printed programs (if needed)
- Invite the Media (if needed)

Chapter 7: Using Social Media to Promote Your Event

There are 5 simple ways you can engage with your audience, promote and sell tickets to your event through social media. Try the following:

Create a FB, Instagram and Twitter account - promote your own branded content organically or with a paid advertising budget

Get involved with social media influencers - promote your brand through the influencers' content organically or with a paid sponsorship

Connect with partners - promote your event and brand through their social networks and email lists

Setup a Lead Generation Campaign - all social media platforms allow you to set up paid campaigns to collect the name, email and phone number of people who may be interested in attending or just hearing more about your event

Sell Direct - You can use your own social media accounts to raise awareness and ask people to buy tickets directly on your landing page or website.

Remember: When it comes to social media advertising, you can pay for it or you can do it yourself and gain organic traction. Organic traction usually takes a lot longer and more of your time to create content and post and engage, tag, use hashtags for discovery etc. Paid advertising will allow you to get your event information out to the public quicker, get buyers pretty fast, but will cost you a pretty penny in advertising spend.

If you decide to use organic social media to promote your event, here are your options:

You can create a facebook, instagram, twitter account. Send out daily messages and reminders, ask for signups, promote discount offers, promote event videos, promote event faqs and information, share behinds the scenes videos, promote group discounts, promote a contest or a giveaway, promote the speakers that are at the event, promote any special activities you have going on. ***Ask your followers to share and like your media.*** You'll need to go in everyday and engage with your audience

In order to drive traffic to your registration page or website. Facebook also allows you to set up a ***free event page*** to put your ticketing link front and center.

Get involved with social media influencers. They can and will promote your brand through their own content. Some ***will do it for free*** in exchange for a vip experience, upgraded or free ticket to your event.

Find other companies or non-for-profits who align with your brand's event strategy and ask them to partner with you. Allow them ***exclusive advertising benefits*** free of charge at your event, and use this partnership as leverage to obtain promotions through their networks and to their followers.

Set up a form on your social media pages for people to ask for more information or inquire about ticket prices. Every post you share should ***drive interest*** towards filling out the lead form.

Search the social media platforms for relevant groups in your niche and share a post about your upcoming invite and invite members of the group to register for more information on your event.

If you decide to use paid social media to promote your event, here are your options:

Setup a Facebook, Instagram, and Twitter ad account to promote your event and drive traffic directly to your event page. You can do a photo ad, an eye catching video or simply text ad.

Include a direct call to action like "Buy Tickets". So people know where they are going when they click the button. Cost is usually set up by a cost per click basis or per lead generated. The price will vary by demographic targeting and location.

You can also use Snapchat or Linkedin to post ads depending on your target. Facebook ads can be used to retarget people who didn't buy the first time around, you can easily send out follow up offers throughout the internet with retargeting.

Get involved with social media influencers. Find influencers in your niche or local area that would like to be paid to create content or promote your event for payment. This website Izea.com can help you find paid influencers.

Find media websites to buy advertising space in their email blasts and on their website. They will co-promote you and send your event registration out to their followers and people in their network for a fair price.

Set up a lead generation campaign directly on social media. People who are interested in attending your event never even have to leave their social media, they simply click a button, put in their name and email address and hit submit.

You'll need to follow up via email or phone call after to close the deal and give them the information they're looking for.

Chapter 8: Best Ways to Generate More Money on Event Day

Remember your goal is to profit from these events. In order to do that, you'll need to generate as much revenue as possible. Make your event worth it by doing the following on event day:

Selling merchandise (shirts, signed posters, calendars, bracelets, headbands etc) is one of the number one ways to get more money on event day. People tend to want a piece of memorabilia from the event.

Sell access to the data / lead information to the registered businesses or event sponsors at the end of the very end of the event

Sell access to wifi at the registration / ticketing desk

Sell tickets / wristbands to an exclusive after party or meet and greet

Sell ticketing seating upgrades (general, vip, super vip)

Sell concierge service with food delivery to your seat or priority seating

Sell discounted companion passes with each ticket

Sell access to onsite lounge area for wifi use, drinks and networking

Sell locker storage for large bags or coats

Have a few ATM's on site for event day to make money off the transaction fees

Chapter 9: Event Marketing Resources

Theme Forest - This website has the best event and conference website templates to get you started. They are easy to use and to edit. They even sell a service that can help you customize the templates.

Here's a List of Useful Templates by style:

Event & Conference Website Designs Under $100

Event Video Promos under $50

Event Music & Audio Clips under $25

Event Flyers, Posters and Graphics

Event Logos

Fiverr - This website has plenty of freelancers that will help you organize, and promote your event.

Here's a List of Useful Event Gigs:

Event Flyer Design Service

Event Planning Service

Event Promo Video Creation

Appendix: "Event Marketing FAQs"

Q: Do I need an event planner or can I realistically do this myself?

A: If you are good at coordination, highly motivated and self directed, I would highly recommend you give it a go. If you struggle with communicating or maybe just need a bit more support on the marketing side of things, it's not uncommon to bring in a marketing or sales team to help expedite the process. It will only benefit you.

Q: What kind of promotional offers should I include for my events?

A: Buy one ticket, get half off 2nd, Free Merchandise with Ticket Purchase, Free VIP upgrade, Free Priority Access Line, Free Autographed Item, Free take home tote bag, early bird tickets, participate in the spin to win game, come to celebrity meet and greet, win an apple tv, get a visa or starbucks gift card with each purchase, special private after party event, flash / limited time offer sale, discounted product offers, loyalty points towards next event or online partner services, buy more save more, extra 20% off when you buy X dollar amount.

**Q: What's the difference between an event planner and a venue /
site coordinator?**

A: Event planners will do a full outline and help you create a full event experience from start to end. This usually includes venue, staffing, logistics, setup and breakdown and payment arrangement. A venue the site coordinator usually introduces you to the venue, tells you their offerings and lets you choose independently.

Appendix: "Event Marketing FAQs"

Q: How often should I send emails to leads / prospects about buying a ticket ?

A: Send it as often as people want or expect to hear from you. That could be one email a day, every morning, or it could be once a week. I wouldn't recommend anything more than once a day or a few times a week. Too many can start to get annoying and increase unsubscribes.

Q: How can planning ahead help me?

A: You will want to stay on top of everything going on involving the event, be sure to track deliverables and allow yourself enough time for marketing and getting the word out to people who may want to attend.

Q: Does everyone need to be paid upfront?

A: Usually the event venue requires a 50% deposit to hold your date and the rest due on or before the actual date of the event. Each vendor will have a specific set of payment requirements, so simply ask and follow up in order to plan your budget accordingly.

Q: Why is hosting an event important?

A: Events are important because they allow for an intimate and engaging experience with your prospects or current customers. This will leave a memorable long lasting impression and is better than any traditional form of advertising.

Appendix B: Recommended Resources

Email Marketing - Aweber

The world's best email marketing software for event marketing newsletters and auto-responders! Create emails with style and get more messages delivered fast! Create professional and powerful email marketing today.

Get a Free Trial of Aweber for Event Marketing

Web Hosting - Bluehost

I highly recommend using Bluehost for your event website. They have an incredibly easy to use 1-click automatic word press installation and amazing customer service. The link below gets you a special discount off the regular price!

Get a 30 Day Money Back Guarantee for a New Website

Business Incorporation - MyCorporation

Everything you need to start, maintain and protect your business. Easily form a corporation or Limited Liability Company in no time. Learn which entity is best for your business!

Legally Incorporate Your Event Business Today

Appendix B: Recommended Resources

Event Supply Purchases - Amazon Business

Create a free Amazon Business account to save time and money on business purchases with competitive B2B prices and discounts. Satisfy your sourcing requirements and get Tax-exempt purchasing.

Get Discounted Supplies with Amazon for Business

Event Logos and Marketing Materials - 99designs

In the past, I have trusted them with logo and website designs. You can use them for all sorts of projects like packaging, email marketing designs, banner ads, business cards, trade show material and more.

Get Logos & Event Marketing Materials Designed Today

Credit Card & Payment Processing - Square

Square helps millions of event companies run their business from secure credit card processing to point of sale solutions. Get paid faster with Square. Sign up today!

Signup for Square for Business

About the Author

MARKETING EXPERT | BRAND STRATEGIST | BUSINESS
COACH | TV HOST

This Business Coach and Marketing Expert has shared her passion for growing brands from the ground up. She's worked with Startups, Small Businesses, Fortune 500 Corporations and entertainment talent that recognize the value of marketing. She gives her clients the ability to access their niche market via online, social media, mobile, merchandising, and events.

The What's Your Game Plan Show features free expert advice and growth strategies for Business Owners and Executives across the globe.

Access thousands of FREE Tips, Trends and Tools to Move Your Business Forward! Contact the author:

AdellaPasos.com
Subscribe to Business Strategy TV Youtube

Made in the USA
Las Vegas, NV
13 November 2020